The Songs Of Salt & Ink

Unspoken Words, Unfinished Stories

Aniket Kumar

BookLeaf
Publishing

India | USA | UK

Made with ❤ on the BookLeaf Publishing Platform
www.bookleafpub.in
www.bookleafpub.com

Dedication

This book is for the ones who have loved and lost, who have searched and stumbled, who have held on and let go. For those who have felt the weight of unspoken words and the ache of unfinished stories.

It's for the quiet battles fought in the mind, the resilience that often goes unnoticed, and the moments of clarity that come when least expected. May these words remind you that no feeling is final, no journey is without meaning, and no heart is truly alone in what it carries.

To the one holding these pages, if somewhere in these verses you find a fragment of yourself, know that you are not alone, that you have a quiet companion on the days when silence feels too loud.

And if they bring even a moment of solace, a flicker of understanding, or the comfort of knowing that someone, somewhere, has felt the same, then this book has found its purpose.

Preface

Poetry has a way of capturing what prose often cannot - the fleeting emotions, the quiet aches, the moments that slip between words. This book is a collection of such moments, woven from memories, reflections, and the raw, unfiltered depths of the heart.

Some of these poems are born from personal experiences, others from the echoes of things left unsaid. They hold love and loss, longing and resilience, hope and surrender. They are not just stories; they are fragments of life - mine, yours, and perhaps of those we've never met but somehow understand.

This book is not meant to instruct or conclude. It is simply meant to be felt. There are no answers here, only emotions laid bare, waiting for you to find your own meaning within them. If, in these pages, you discover a thought you've once had, a feeling you've buried, or a truth you've been searching for, then these words have done what they were meant to do.

Take your time. Read, pause, revisit. And above all, feel.

Acknowledgements

As I reflect on the journey of this book, it is impossible to separate the words within these pages from the almighty, the people and moments that brought them to life.

To Lord Shiva - the eternal source of strength, wisdom, and destruction of illusions. In the chaos and in the calm, in the unanswered questions and the quiet realizations, your presence has always been my guiding force.

To my family - your unwavering love, patience, and quiet strength have always been my anchor. Even in silence, you understood what words couldn't express.

To my friends - thank you for being my sounding boards, my late-night confidants, and my safe space. Your presence, whether near or far, has meant everything. You have been the muses that have shaped this book, sometimes with a single conversation or a moment of shared laughter.

To those who crossed my path, even briefly - some of you stayed, some of you left, but all of you left something behind. In lessons, in memories, in echoes of conversations, I carry you in these pages.

To the readers - this book is no longer just mine; it is yours now. If even a single line resonates with you, if a single verse makes you pause, then every word has been worth it.

And finally, to the unwritten, the unsaid, and the unanswered - perhaps some things are meant to live between the lines.

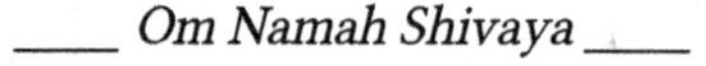

_____ *Om Namah Shivaya* _____

Dream To Be

The town lay quiet, wrapped in the hush of noon,
Air thick as syrup, slow and swoon.
Dust curled in restless swirls on the street,
Even the trees drooped in the heavy heat.

Three summers had passed, each one the same,
Days of longing, whispering a name.
Hopes were woven, then left to fray,
Yet faith stood firm, come what may.

Then like the hush before the rain,
Like cool hands on fevered skin,
A moment arrived, soft yet bright,
Turning heat to golden light.

He sat quiet, hands clenched tight,
She breathed a prayer in the dim-lit light.
Three years of waiting, three years of dreams,
Folded now in silent beams.

Then laughter rang, unbridled, free,
A tide that crashed, a swelling sea.
Eyes met eyes, brimming bright,
The world reborn in early twilight.

The heat still clung, the town still slept,
Yet joy like rain through windows crept.
For what was thirst, what was pain,
When hearts had danced in love again?

That night, beneath a sky so wide,
They held a vow, hearts open, tied.
To nurture, to guide, through dark and light,
To shape a soul, both strong and right.

No riches claimed, no thrones were sought,
Just love enough, a world well-wrought.
With hands so firm, yet soft and free,
They whispered, "You will be all you dream to be."

The Night So Dark

Night whispered in echoes of fading songs.
A reel of colors, a world now gone.
The cold clung soft to the empty streets.
Midnight stretched long, the town half-asleep.

They walked home, warmth still in their voices,
Movie melodies looping in their minds.
A child waited inside, small and safe,
His world no bigger than their embrace.

The air was thick with the scent of warmth,
Soft hands tore, passed, fed.
Perched too high, his feet swung free,
A moment too quick -

A shift.
A slip.
A sharp breath.

Then sound, metal, bone, the crack of time splitting open.

Scarlet bloomed on the cold, hard floor.
The room shrank.
His father's hands trembled.
His mother's voice cracked into a thousand prayers.

The night was no longer soft.

Arms lifted, tight, desperate.
Thin fabric clung to skin, unready for the cold.
Bare feet against stone,
Racing past locked doors, silent homes.

The streets blurred.
A steel gate rattled open.
Light spilled harsh and white,
The smell of antiseptic and midnight prayers.

Hands pressed together, shaking, pleading.
A whisper, "Do something."
A cry swallowed before it could break.

Somewhere, a clock kept moving.
Somewhere, the world still turned.
But in that room, time stood still,
Hinged on a breath that wouldn't come.

Shadows stretched across pale walls,

bodies curled into silent prayers.
A hand gripped too tight, knuckles white,
whispering names only the heavens could hear.

The night refused to end.
Seconds dragged, folding into hours,
stitched together with quiet sobs
and the hum of machines counting breaths.

A temple formed in that waiting room,
not of stone, nor brass, nor bells,
only trembling lips and tear-stained hands,
offering nothing but hope.

And then -

A flicker.
A shift.
A breath that finally came back home.

Eyes that had forgotten sleep blinked in disbelief.
Relief did not come as a flood,
but as a slow trickle,
hesitant, afraid to trust.

Fingers traced a bandaged wound,
as if to be sure, as if to promise,

Never again.
Not if the world had to be moved,
not if the stars had to be begged.

Outside, the night had exhaled.
The cold still clung, but the world felt softer,
as two souls sat beside a sleeping child,
watching over him as if he might disappear.

They would never speak of this night.
But they would carry it, always.

First Prayer Answered

I wished for you with all my might,
A sister's love, pure and bright.
And when you came, my heart just knew,
My world was whole because of you.

Your tiny hands, your toothy grin,
The joy you brought, the laughs within.
I'd spin my tricycle round and round,
Just to hear your giggles sound.

Oh, the trouble I would find,
For all the pranks and acts unkind!
But every scolding, every fall,
Was worth it, for you, through all.

You stole my time, you stole my space,
Yet left a love I can't replace.
My secret keeper, my dearest guide,
My closest friend, my greatest pride.

We shared our dreams, our joys, our fears,
Our whispered talks through childhood years.
And when I left, you stood alone,
Yet stayed so strong, so fully grown.

I saw you fight, I saw you rise,
Through shattered dreams and hopeful skies.
And though the world may shift and bend,
You'll always have your truest friend.

For come what may, come joy or fall,
You are my heart, my soul, my all.
And in this life, one thing stays true,
No bond on earth can match me & you.

Crumpled Papers

The mornings were battles, sleepy-eyed wars,
Shoes left untied, the school bag ajar.
A honking auto, the hurried goodbyes,
With dreams of home still in my eyes.

The classroom smelled of chalk and air,
Of scribbled notes and vacant stares.
The teacher's gaze, so sharp, so keen,
Caught us mid-whisper, where we'd been.

Two boys stood waiting by the door,
Punishment never felt like a chore.
A smirk, a nudge, the time passed fast,
As we turned our crime into a laugh.

Some pages torn, some words erased,
A lesson learned, a trial faced.
Another voice, so stern, so loud,
Accused me of twisting the truth around.

But mother's fire burned bright and high,
No room for deceit, no place for a lie.
Her words cut through like sharpened steel,
Making sure the world would feel,
That trust was stitched into my name,
And no red mark could bring me shame.

Then came the winter, cruel and long,
Fevered nights and silent songs.
A heavy spell held me to rest,
While outside, the world ran its test.

But races called, the ground felt near,
A scraped-up knee, a wiped-off tear.
Falling, rising, pushing through,
That's what little boys must do.

And then, a stumble, but not the same,
A fall into laughter, into a name.
A voice so bright, her eyes so deep,
That played between the desks and me.

We sang, we laughed, we stole the day,
In secret tunes that wouldn't stay.
A childhood crush, so light, so fleet,
Like paper boats on rainy streets.

The bell rang loud, the years soon passed,
Yet echoes of the past still last.
A boy still runs, still stumbles, still dreams,
Tucked in the folds of old routines.
And in his pocket, crumpled tight,
Are stories of a time still bright.

Lessons Beyond the Classroom

The year was a rhythm, steady and bright,
Laughter in corridors, lessons in flight.
A drum in my hands, a badge on my chest,
Marching in tune, giving my best.

Winter arrived, the holidays called,
A home in the countryside, strong and old.
Cricket in dust, barefooted runs,
Chiding voices, but endless fun.

Stories at dusk, wrapped in his tone,
A transistor hummed of days long gone.
Walks in the chill, footprints in dew,
Mornings that felt untouched and new.

Then came the night, still and unkind,
A phone call that silenced time.
Frozen stares, words unsaid,
A pillar of life, suddenly fled.

By the riverside, where farewells burned,
Hands in the sand, the world unturned.
Too young to mourn, too old to play,
Grief didn't arrive the usual way.

And then, a silence, deeper still,
As love refused the loss to fill.
One heart followed, as if in vow,
Two names etched in memory now.

Exams knocked, life didn't wait,
Pages turned beneath their weight.
Numb hands wrote, a mind stayed true,
Somehow, I did what I had to do.

A medal, an honor, a fleeting cheer,
Yet joy and sorrow blurred that year.
For life had whispered, soft yet stern,
Some lessons books will never learn.

The Stolen Secret

The library card felt like a key,
Unlocking worlds unknown to me.
Through yellowed pages, I would slip,
Into mysteries, into ships,
Where footsteps creaked on wooden floors,
And secrets hid behind locked doors.

That day, the lesson was morality,
But I was lost in another tale.
Eyes tracing clues, chasing thieves,
As justice tipped the justice scale.
A shadow passed, too late to hide,
A piercing voice, a book denied.

The whack came down, the class went still,
My name, a whisper, a sharp-edged thrill.
A girl stood up, her voice was kind,
But shame had wrapped around my mind.
And so, the weight of words unsaid
Made tears slip out, though none were read.

The punishment was set, the price was clear,
Yet cost was feeble than the fear,
That night, with quiet, careful hands,
I stole to settle what I'd lost.
No locks were forced, no glass was shattered,
Yet something deep inside felt battered.

The years moved on, the secret stayed,
A hidden tale, a debt unpaid.
Until one day, in quiet air,
I told them all, I laid it bare.
No scolding came, no judgment fell,
Just time uncoiling from its shell.

And though they smiled, I felt it then,
A wish that someone, way back when,
Had seen beyond the guilty glance,
Had known the passion within the chance.

Because sometimes, all a child needs
Is not just rules, not just decrees,
But someone who can truly see,
The fire lit by poetry.

Shadows of a Mistake

It started as laughter, a harmless game,
A quick little prank, no one to blame.
A pen placed under a careless seat,
A wince, a chuckle, our mischief complete.

But jokes have echoes, ripples spread,
And what came next, I still dread.
A sharper trick, a pointed reply,
Beneath me lay the reason why.

The pencil snapped, the pain ran deep,
Carried away, I tried not to weep.
Hands searched, tweezers found,
A wound now stitched, a lesson unbound.

A nod, a word, a name set free,
Two boys punished because of me.
One was sent, never to return,
And in my chest, regret would burn.

Why didn't I speak, why didn't I say,
That I, too, had set this play?
Fear held tight, guilt held long,
The right was lost between the wrong.

Years have passed, but still I find,
Mistakes haunt the cautious mind.
I double-check, I hesitate,
Afraid that errors seal my fate.

If only schools had taught us then,
That mistakes don't define good men.
That courage blooms where truth is sown,
And mercy makes us truly grown.

Walls that watched us Grow

The door creaked one last time,
as footsteps lingered on fading floors.
Walls, once filled with laughter and mischief,
stood still, holding echoes of days no more.

A tricycle rolling, a tiny hand offering greens,
a father's stories, a mother's calls,
soft whispers of love and lessons,
woven deep into peeling walls.

The narrow corridor knew my cricket shots,
the road below knew my gaze.
I watched squirrels chase the seasons,
and kites cut loose in fiery haze.

Festivals burst in color and light,
Diwali's glow, Sankranti's flight.
Summer nights on an endless sky,
counting stars with sleepy eyes.

Then came the day of packed-up pasts,
boxes stacked, the goodbye fast.
A house left standing, memories intact,
but a childhood carried to where we sat.

The new walls felt empty, too clean, too bare,
the streets unfamiliar, the air too rare.
But time, like a quiet friend unseen,
taught me to belong, taught me to dream.

New laughter filled forgotten space,
new friends, new games, new chase.
Yet somewhere in shadows, I still know,
those walls still watch, as I still grow.

The Notes We Shared

The last bells rang, the corridors hummed,
With laughter, plans, and footsteps drummed.
Two years slipped by like a whispered tune,
Carrying echoes of a time too soon.

A notebook passed, a debt repaid,
Her lessons to me, my words relayed.
Ink and pages, a quiet exchange,
A language of youth, both new and strange.

I never said it, she never asked,
Yet somehow, in moments, the silence basked.
A borrowed smile, a fleeting glance,
A rhythm wrapped in circumstance.

Practice fields and broken beats,
Dreams once marched, now took their seat.
A lesson in leaving, in letting go,
Of sticks, of drums, of things we know.

Then came the days of ink and dread,
Numbers danced inside my head.
The city woke before the dawn,
And I was gone before it yawned.

The hall was cold, the benches long,
Papers waiting to prove me wrong.
Yet every tick, every breath,
Felt like a step towards what came next.

And when it ended, when the ink had dried,
A sigh escaped, a silent pride.
The numbers smiled, the scores stood tall,
And I stood ready to take it all.

Some books were left,
some dreams were spared,
But I still remember,
The notes we shared.

A Betrayal Without Words

The air was still, the room so tight,
A battle lost without a fight.
His gaze was firm, his voice so clear,
"Admit it now, or disappear."

Outside the door, two stood in shame,
Their silence whispered I'd do the same.
I met their eyes, but they looked away,
Had they too chosen not to stay?

I thought of him, my friend, so true,
The laughs we shared, the trials we knew.
Through every storm, through every fall,
We swore to stand, we swore through all.

But fear crept in with quiet tread,
It wrapped around the words unsaid.
I took the pen, I signed the line,
And let them call the guilt as mine.

The next day came, his desk stood bare,
His name a ghost upon the air.
No trace remained, no whisper stayed,
As if the past could just be swayed.

And I remained, with hollow pride,
A truth I buried deep inside.
For what I chose, I can't undo,
A friend betrayed, a self lost too.

Lantern Nights

The pages blurred, the nights were long,
A whispered dream kept me strong.
A lantern's glow, a quiet fight,
To turn the dark into light.

From second place, I took a fall,
Chemistry made no sense at all.
Sixteen marks, a bitter sting,
A mind once sharp now wandering.

Then came a guide, so young yet wise,
Who saw the spark behind my eyes.
He built me up from roots so weak,
Till numbers danced, and bonds could speak.

The city slept, but I would rise,
At dawn, with dreams that touched the skies.
Through books and notes, through highs and lows,
The fire within just seemed to grow.

By day, the school; by dusk, the grind,
A race against my troubled mind.
Physics soared, and math felt right,
While Chemistry turned dark to bright.

Then came the test, the final stand,
A pen, a desk, a trembling hand.
The doubts were there, but so was will,
And every lesson echoed still.

The scores arrived, a shining feat,
The past lay crumbled at my feet.
Just shy of gold, yet proud I stayed,
For I had won the war I'd waged.

So now I know, when storms arise,
And shadows loom in weary skies,
That in the darkest, toughest fight,
A lantern's glow can bring the light.

Forged in Fire

The papers lay, the ink ran dry,
A dream so big, a heart held high.
Yet numbers ruled, and fate was grim,
A three-mark chasm, a future dim.

The halls were loud, the air was tight,
Yet I had hoped, I'd fought my fight.
The gates had closed, the chance was gone,
But I refused to be withdrawn.

A new path carved, a second start,
With borrowed hope and a burning heart.
Yet when I knocked on doors for aid,
Their smiles were masks, their words were blades.

"A dream too big," my own blood said,
"Stay where you are, choose this instead."
Their pockets full, their hands so bare,
Yet not an ounce of love to spare.

But fire is born from bitter cold,
From debts unpaid and dreams unsold.
A mother's gold, a father's land,
They gave me wings with trembling hands.

And so I swore, beneath that sky,
That none like me would be denied.
One day I'd stand, so strong, so tall,
That need would never break us all.

Every Quiet Victory

I stepped on cracked stone with hopeful eyes,
Where wild grass grew and monkeys swung by.
A jungle, they said, yet I stayed,
For something in me still loved the shade.

Hostel walls echoed with names and jokes,
Wingmates loud, the corridor smoked.
One watched cartoons, one crooned old songs,
In their madness, I found where I belonged.

The rooms were small, the dreams were wide,
With midnight walks and snacks on the side.
We fought for bandwidth, lived on memes,
Bunked our lectures, chased wild dreams.

One afternoon, beneath humming lights,
A smile flickered, soft and bright.
The air grew warmer, wires went still,
And silence spoke what I couldn't spill.

Some bonds bloomed, some thin, some deep,
Some left a mark, some went to sleep.
They came like seasons, bright then gone,
But echoes of them still linger on.

We bunked some classes, danced in the rain,
Played dumb charades, acted insane.
From riverside prayers to fest-lit nights,
We dreamed aloud under hostel lights.

Then came a fall, a silence so loud,
A night turned numb beneath a cloud.
We held a hand that would not rise,
And saw the world through a mother's cries.

Yet still, we rose, wore cloaks of flame,
Carved our worth in the world's old frame.
We lit small fires, stumbled through wind,
Shaping slowly who we were within.

A city of echoes, of trams and tales,
Where steam rose high and resolve derailed.
I walked its veins in monsoon grace,
And found my rhythm, my quiet place.

Came trials wrapped in numbered sheets,
Hushed halls, cold rails, and aching feet.

A few hearts slipped, some moments bled,
But I moved on with dreams I fed.

No spotlight knew the paths I'd crossed,
Each step a win, each bruise a cost.
That shimmer spoke not just of me,
But of every quiet victory.

The Chair That Spun

I came with a bag and a hopeful smile,
To glaring halls, to walk a while.
The badge was new, the dreams were old,
But the heart was young, and quietly bold.

They spoke of systems, training and code,
While I found warmth on a different road.
A room of screens, a corner seat,
Where strangers turned to memories sweet.

We laughed on benches, beneath the trees,
Shared stories, songs, and sips in the breeze.
Talked of stars, of films and fate,
Of all that heals, and all that's late.

But work has ways of drawing lines,
And time keeps turning sacred signs.
She drifted first, or maybe I,
Too much to feel, too much to try.

Some wounds I wrapped in silent thread,
Some words I wished I never said.
But love that clings without a name,
Is bound to break beneath the flame.

I found escape in a different fight,
In virtual wars deep into night.
A clan, a crown, a quiet pride,
As battles raged and sleep just died.

Then came a test, a seat, a screen,
No pressure loud, no urgent dream.
But calm can crack what stress might fake,
And I gave more than I meant to take.

A number blinked, my world stood still,
The start of rise from quiet will.
Calls rolled in, one after the other,
Felt like I could hug the sky, or my mother.

Laughter burst from a silent place,
I wheeled around in sudden grace,
The chair that spun beneath my cry,
A moment I still hold close and high.

She tried again, but I had grown,
The lies were loud, the trust long gone.

No wounds to nurse, no hearts to mend,
Just a chapter closed, a clean-cut end.

And now I stood at a different gate,
With lighter bags and kinder fate.
My name on walls I'd only dreamed,
A life ahead that finally gleamed.

The past was tough, but it led me here,
To courage found beyond the fear.
A second chance, a sky so wide,
And something in me burned with pride.

I looked ahead, I felt it then,
The start of all I'd hoped to gain.
The nights were real, the days were long,
But I had made it through the rain.

The Hallowed Years

June arrived with skies of gold,
And I stepped through gates untold.
A place of whispers, dreams set free,
Where echoes hum of what could be.

Seven lakes held secrets deep,
Under canopies where lost hearts meet.
Friendships sparked in moonlit halls,
Laughter danced along the walls.

Days unfurled in hurried streams,
Pages turned, yet slipped like dreams.
The chase was swift, the climb was steep,
And some desires we could not keep.

Between the madness, moments stayed,
A touch, a glance, a vow half-made.
By quiet waters, fate would weave,
A love so soft, yet bound to leave.

The next year, a gentler tide,
With stolen hours, and hands untried.
Midnight feasts, a gambler's thrill,
Long debates and friendships still.

Then came the day the echoes dimmed,
The halls still stood, yet something thinned.
A final glance, a sigh, a tear,
What once was home was far from near.

Yet, even now, when silence calls,
The laughter hums within those walls.
It was never just the place we knew,
But the souls that lived, the dreams that grew.

Grit and Grace

A door swung open, a path laid wide,
From lessons learned to a journey untied.
A chance was given, a dream took flight,
Into a world where visions ignite.

Different paths, new worlds to roam,
New faces, new places, a life from home.
Boarding gates and fleeting stays,
Ideas shaped in endless days.

Then came the world of screens and scrolls,
Designs that spoke, pixels with soul.
Not just a plan, but hands in clay,
Molding the brand in a bold new way.

A canvas stretched, a vision grew,
Patterns and textures, something new.
Not all dreams meet the sky,
Yet footprints stay when we dare to try.

Now hands extend to those who build,
To forge their trust, to have them willed.
A challenge vast, yet filled with spark,
To shape a story, to leave a mark.

Beyond the work, a home was found,
With bonds of trust, both firm and sound.
Through storms of life, through highs and lows,
A steady hand, a light that glows.

Some days we run, some days we crawl,
Not every climb is tall or small.
Yet even when the path is blurred,
A step ahead is a step forward.

May this journey keep its grace,
With strength regained, I'll find my pace.
To give my best, to rise, to grow,
To meet the heights I've yet to know.

Three Journeys, One Soul

In days of youth, when time stood still,
We chased the winds to a distant hill.
Laughter echoed, water fell free,
A farewell hymn to our years carefree.
We swam, we climbed, we played, we ran,
The world was ours, no future plan.
And though the roads held moments tight,
Our hearts still soared with endless light.

Then came the days of suits and screens,
Lost in work, caught in routines.
Yet mist-clad heights began to call,
Where cliffs and echoes held us all.
The valleys hid in clouds so white,
A road trip filled with sheer delight.
We sang, we laughed, we breathed so deep,
For once, awake from corporate sleep.

But oh, the peaks of lands untold,
Where time bows down and hearts unfold.

A temple perched on mountain steep,
Held whispers from the monks so deep.
The air so pure, the rivers wide,
The peace of mountains side by side.
A place so calm, so vast, so new,
I dreamt of staying, losing view.

Through hills and valleys, fog and streams,
These journeys shape my wandering dreams.
For nature's call, so wild, so free,
Still writes its verses deep in me.
Each step I take, each path I tread,
A poet's heart forever led.

Echoes of Us

I built a house where love could stay,
With careful hands, in my own way.
Brick by brick, I laid it true,
Yet never saw it was built for two.

You spoke in waves, I spoke in stone,
We stood together, yet felt alone.
You searched for warmth in a wintered touch,
I gave you all, but not enough.

Through crowded rooms, I called your name,
But silence answered just the same.
I reached for you in quiet nights,
But found a shadow, dimmed of light.

Storms arrived, as storms will do,
I braved them all, I thought you knew.
Yet when the sky began to break,
You were the first the winds would take.

Love should mend, but ours unspooled,
A thread too tight, a thread too pulled.
And so, we stood where endings start,
Two strangers lost in the same heart.

Still, echoes hum where laughter grew,
A life once ours, now split in two.
No anger left, no words to say,
Just love that learned to walk away.

Rolling Down The Lane

Late at night, I twist, I turn,
Sleep eludes, and memories burn.
Echoes call from days long past,
Fading slow, yet holding fast.
I close my eyes, yet drift again,
Departing, rolling down the lane.

Mornings once had softer hues,
Dreams unchained, with nothing to lose.
Steps were light, the world felt wide,
The road was long, but safe inside.

Laughter rang where echoes fade,
Footsteps danced, yet fears were made.
Chased and stumbled, lost and found,
Fell too deep, yet stood my ground.

Autumn came and stripped it bare,
Winds of change hung in the air.
What once was bright had turned to dust,

Yet moving on was still a must.

Now night recedes, the dawn remains,
A golden hue on window panes.
And as I breathe, alive again,
I find myself rolling down the lane.

The Flame Still Burns

Morning broke in misty hue,
Sunlight pierced the sky so blue.
Clouds were torn, the trees stood tall,
Nature whispered, embracing all.

I walked the path where many tread,
Where dreams were born and often bled.
But when I reached the promised place,
The ground beneath had lost its grace.

A friend once said, "Don't doubt the way,
Or your own dreams will drift away."
So I turned, left roads behind,
Chased new paths with fate unkind.

I climbed the steps, I aimed so high,
But fog had blurred the open sky.
I rose, I fell, I tried again,
Victory whispered through the pain.

Yet at a door, I paused and sighed,
For here I should have stood with pride.
A battle missed, a war still fought,
A dream delayed, a lesson taught.

Now memories laugh, they cry, they call,
Of wins and wounds, I keep them all.
Through highs and lows, my spirit learns,
Through all of it, the flame still burns.

Whisper To The Cosmos

Sometimes I dream, sometimes I stray,
Sometimes I fight, sometimes I sway.
Sometimes I wish I could shift and bend,
Yet in my heart, I stay the same.

The earth, the waves, the air so light,
The fire that flickers, fierce and bright.
They call my soul, they pull me near,
They hum a song I ache to hear.

The ground I tread is no mere dust,
It bears my weight, it holds my trust.
I toil, I falter, yet still, I stand,
For unseen hands conceal the sand.

The tides rise high, then sink below,
They cleanse, they cradle, they let me go.
If only I could drift away,
A fleeting wave, a rolling sway.

The wind that whispers through the trees,
Sings untamed songs upon the seas.
A voice not mine, yet in my ear,
It soothes, it stays, it draws me near.

And fire, wild, untamed, divine,
A force that burns, yet gives its shine.
It rages high, then turns to embers,
A dance of all my lost Decembers.

If I could be a breath, a spark,
A sliver of light within the dark.
A grain of sand, a drop, a flame,
Yet still, unshaken, still the same.

Oh, how I long to rise and stand,
To reach, to hold, to lend a hand.